CW00665976

Thoughts I Met on th

Words of Friendly Cheer From
"The Life Books"

Ralph Waldo Trine

Alpha Editions

This edition published in 2023

ISBN : 9789357949255

Design and Setting By
Alpha Editions
www.alphaedis.com
Email - info@alphaedis.com

Contents

THOUGHTS I MET ON THE HIGHWAY WORDS OF FRIENDLY CHEER FROM "THE LIFE BOOKS"

Thoughts are forces—like builds like and like attracts like. Thoughts of strength both build strength from within and attract it from without. Thoughts of weakness actualize weakness from within and attract it from without. Courage begets strength, fear begets weakness. And so courage begets success, fear begets failure.

Any way the old world goes
Happy be the weather!
With the red thorn or the rose
Singin' all together!
Don't you see that sky o' blue!
Good Lord painted it for you
Reap the daisies in the dew
Singin' all together!
Springtime sweet, an' frosty fall
Happy be the weather!
Earth has gardens for us all,
Goin' on together.

Sweet the labor in the light,
To the harvest's gold and white—
Till the toilers say "Good night,"
Singin' all together!

There is no quality that exerts more good, is of greater service to all mankind during the course of the ordinary life, than the mind and the heart that goes out in an all-embracing love for all, that is the generator and the circulator of a genuine, hearty, wholesome sympathy and courage and good cheer, that is not disturbed or upset by the passing occurrence little or great, but that is serene, tranquil, and conquering to the end, that is looking for the best, that is finding the best, and that is inspiring the best in all. There is moreover, no quality that when genuine brings such rich returns to its possessor by virtue of the thoughts and the feelings that it inspires and calls forth from others and that come back laden with their peaceful, stimulating, healthful influences for you.

Out of the night that covers me,
Black as the Pit from pole to pole,
I thank whatever gods may be
For my unconquerable soul.

In the fell clutch of circumstance
I have not winced nor cried aloud.
Under the bludgeoning of chance
My head is bloody, but unbowed.

Beyond this place of wrath and tears
Looms but the horror of the shade,
And yet the menace of the years
Finds and shall find me, unafraid.

It matters not how strait the gate
How charged with punishment the scroll,
I am the master of my fate;
I am the captain of my soul.

William Earnest Henley

Thought is the great builder in human life: it is the determining factor. Continually think thoughts that are good, and your life will show forth in goodness, and your body in health and beauty. Continually think evil thoughts, and your life will show forth in evil, and your body in weakness and repulsiveness. Think thoughts of love, and you will love and will be loved. Think thoughts of hatred, and you will hate and will be hated. Each follows its kind.

Every day is a fresh beginning,
Every morning is the world made new;
You who are weary of sorrow and sinning,
Here is a beautiful hope for you,
A hope for me and a hope for you.

All the past things are past and over,
The tasks are done, and the tears are shed.
Yesterday's errors let yesterday cover;
Yesterday's wounds, which smarted and bled,
Are healed with the healing which night has shed.

Every day is a fresh beginning,
Listen, my soul, to the glad refrain,
And, spite of old sorrow and older sinning,
And puzzles forecasted, and possible pain,
Take heart with the day and begin again.

Each morning is a fresh beginning. We are, as it were, just beginning life. We have it *entirely* in our own hands. And when the morning with its fresh beginning comes, all yesterdays should be yesterdays, with which we have nothing to do. Sufficient is it to know that the way we lived our yesterday has determined for us our today. And, again, when the morning with its fresh beginning comes, all tomorrows should be tomorrows, with which we have nothing to do. Sufficient to know that the way we live our today determines our tomorrow.

Simply the first hour of this new day, with all its richness and glory, with all its sublime and eternity-determining possibilities, and each succeeding hour as it comes, but *not before* it comes—

this is the secret of character building. This simple method will bring any one to the realization of the highest life that can be even conceived of, and there is nothing in this connection that can be conceived of that cannot be realized somehow, somewhen, somewhere.

The poem hangs on the berry-bush
When comes the poet's eye,
And the whole street is a masquerade
When Shakespeare passes by.

This same Shakespeare, whose mere passing causes all this commotion, is the one who put into the mouth of one of his creations the words: "The fault, dear Brutus, is not in our stars, but in ourselves, that we are underlings." And again he gave us a great truth when he said:

"Our doubts are traitors,
And make us lose the good we oft might win
By fearing to attempt."

There is probably no agent that brings us more undesirable conditions than fear. We should live in fear of nothing, nor will we when we come fully to know ourselves. An old French proverb runs:

"Some of your griefs you have cured,
And the sharpest you still have survived;
But what torments of pain you endured
From evils that never arrived."

Fear and lack of faith go hand in hand. The one is born of the other. Tell me how much one is given to fear, and I will tell you how much he lacks in faith. Fear is a most expensive guest to entertain, the same as worry is: so expensive are they that no one can afford to entertain them. We invite what we fear, the same as, by a different attitude of mind, we invite and attract the influences and conditions we desire.

To remain in nature always sweet and simple and humble, and therefore strong.

"Whatever the weather may be," says he,
"Whatever the weather may be,
It's the songs ye sing, an' the smiles ye wear,
That's a-makin' the sun shine everywhere."

James Whitcomb Riley

Sweetness of nature, simplicity in manners and conduct, humility without self-abasement, give the truly kingly quality to men, the queenly to women, the winning to children, whatever the rank or the station may be. The life dominated by this characteristic, or rather these closely allied characteristics, is a natural well-spring of joy to itself and sheds a continual benediction upon all who come within the scope of its influence. It makes for a life of great beauty in itself, and it imparts courage and hope and buoyancy to all others.

There is no thing we cannot overcome;
Say not thy evil instinct is inherited,
Or that some trait inborn makes thy whole life forlorn;
And calls down punishment that is not merited.

Back of thy parents and grandparents lies
The Great Eternal Will! That too is thine
Inheritance,—strong, beautiful, divine,
Sure lever of success for one who tries.

Earth has no claim the soul cannot contest;
Know thyself part of the Eternal Source;

Naught can stand before thy spirit's force:
The soul's Divine Inheritance is best.

———————————

Thought is at the bottom of all progress or retrogression, of
all success or failure, of all that is desirable or undesirable in
human life. The type of thought we entertain both creates and
draws conditions that crystallize about it, conditions exactly
the same in nature as is the thought that gives them form.
Thoughts are forces, and each creates of its kind, whether we
realize it or not. The great law of the drawing power of the
mind, which says that like creates like, and that like attracts like,
is continually working in every human life, for it is one of the
great immutable laws of the universe. For one to take time to
see clearly the things one would attain to, and then to hold that
ideal steadily and continually before his mind, never allowing
faith—his positive thought-forces—to give way to or to be
neutralized by doubts and fears, and then to set about doing
each day what his hands find to do, never complaining, but
spending the time that he would otherwise spend in complaint
in focusing his thought-forces upon the ideal that his mind has
built, will sooner or later bring about the full materialization of
that for which he sets out.

———————————

Beauty seen is never lost,
God's colors all are fast;
The glory of this sunset heaven
Into my soul has passed,—
A sense of gladness unconfined
To mortal, date or clime;
As the soul liveth, it shall live
Beyond the years of time.
Beside the mystic asphodels
Shall bloom the home-born flowers,
And new horizons flush and glow
With sunset hues of ours.

Whittier

Would you remain always young, and would you carry all the
joyousness and buoyancy of youth into your maturer years?
Then have care concerning but one thing,—how you live in
your thought world. It was the inspired one, Gautama, the
Buddha, who said,—"The mind is everything; what you think
you become." And the same thing had Ruskin in mind when
he said,—"Make yourselves nests of pleasant thoughts. None
of us as yet know, for none of us have been taught in early
youth, what fairy palaces we may build of beautiful thought—
proof against all adversity." And would you have in your body all
the elasticity, all the strength, all the beauty of your younger
years? Then live these in your mind, making no room for
unclean thought, and you will externalize them in your body.
In the degree that you keep young in thought will you remain
young in body. And you will find that your body will in turn
aid your mind, for body helps mind the same as mind helps
body.

  There is a sacred Something on all ways—
Something that watches through the Universe;
One that remembers, reckons and repays,
Giving us love for love, and curse for curse.

Edwin Markham

The power of every life, the very life itself, is determined by
what it relates itself to. God is immanent as well as
transcendent. He is creating, working, ruling in the universe
today, in your life and in mine, just as much as He ever has
been. We are too apt to regard Him after the manner of an
absentee landlord, one who has set in operation the forces of
this great universe, and then taken Himself away.

In the degree, however, that we recognize Him as immanent as well as transcendent, are we able to partake of His life and power. For in the degree that we recognize Him as the Infinite Spirit of Life and Power that is today, at this very moment, working and manifesting in and through all, and then, in the degree that we come into the realization of our oneness with this life, do we become partakers of, and so do we actualize in ourselves the qualities of his life. In the degree that we open ourselves to the inflowing tide of this immanent and transcendent life, do we make ourselves channels through which the Infinite Intelligence and Power can work.

The robber is robbed by his riches;
The tyrant is dragged by his chain;
The schemer is snared by his cunning,
The slayer lies dead by the slain.

Edwin Markham

This is the law of prosperity: When apparent adversity comes, be not cast down by it, but make the best of it, and always look forward for better things, for conditions more prosperous. To hold yourself in this attitude of mind is to set into operation subtle, silent, and irresistible forces that sooner or later will actualize in material form that which is today merely an idea. But ideas have occult power, and ideas, when rightly planted and rightly tended, are the seeds that actualize material conditions.

Never give a moment to complaint, but utilize the time that would otherwise be spent in this way in looking forward and actualizing the conditions you desire. Suggest prosperity to yourself. See yourself in a prosperous condition. Affirm that you will before long be in a prosperous condition. Affirm it calmly and quietly, but strongly and confidently. Believe it, believe it absolutely. Expect it,—keep it continually watered with expectation. You thus make yourself a magnet to attract the things that you desire. Don't be afraid to suggest.

They might not need me—yet they might,
I'll let my heart be just in sight.
A smile so small as mine might be
Precisely their necessity.

Emily Dickinson

The grander natures and the more thoughtful are always looking for and in conversation dwelling on the better things in others. It is the rule with but few, if any exceptions, that the more noble and worthy and thoughtful the nature, the more it is continually looking for the best there is to be found in every life. Instead of judging or condemning, or acquiring the habit that eventually leads to this, it is looking more closely to and giving its time to living more worthily itself.

It is in this way continually unfolding and expanding in beauty and in power; it is finding an ever-increasing happiness by the admiration and the love that such a life is always, even though all unconsciously, calling to itself from all sources. It is the life that pays by many fold.

We just shake hands at meeting
With many that come nigh
We nod the head in greeting
To many that go by—

But welcome through the gateway
Our few old friends and true;
Then hearts leap up, and straightway
There's open house for you.

Old friends.
There's open house for you!

Gerald Massey

Many times the struggles are greater than we can ever know. We need more gentleness and sympathy and compassion in our common human life. Then we will neither blame nor condemn. Instead of blaming or condemning we will sympathize.

"Comfort one another.
For the way is often dreary
And the feet are often weary,
And the heart is very sad.
There is a heavy burden bearing,
When it seems that none are caring,
And we half forget that ever we were glad.

"Comfort one another
With the hand-clasp close and tender.
With the sweetness love can render,
And the looks of friendly eyes.
Do not wait with grace unspoken,
While life's daily bread is broken—
Gentle speech is oft like manna from the skies."

And then when we fully realize the fact that selfishness is at the root of all error, sin, and crime, and that ignorance is the basis of all selfishness, with what charity we come to look upon the acts of all. It is the ignorant man who seeks his own ends at the expense of the greater whole. It is the ignorant man, therefore, who is the selfish man.

To get up immediately when we stumble, face again to the light, and travel on without wasting even a moment in regret.

We are on the way from the imperfect to the perfect; some day, in this life or some other, we shall reach our destiny. It is as much the part of folly to waste time and cripple our forces in vain, unproductive regrets in regard to the occurences of the past as it is to cripple our forces through fears and forebodings for the future.

There is no experience in any life which if rightly recognized, rightly turned and thereby wisely used, cannot be made of value; many times things thus turned and used can be made sources of inestimable gain; ofttimes they become veritable blessings in disguise.

'Tis the sweetest thing to remember
If courage be on the wane.
When the cold, dark days are over—
Why, the birds go north again.

Ella Higginson

Nothing is more subtle than thought, nothing more powerful, nothing more irresistible in its operations, when rightly applied and held to with a faith and fidelity that is unswerving,—a faith and fidelity that never knows the neutralizing effects of doubt and fear. If one have aspirations and a sincere desire for a higher and better condition, so far as advantages, facilities, associates, or any surroundings or environments are concerned, and if he continually send out his highest thought forces for the realization of these desires, and continually water these forces with firm expectation as to their fulfillment, he will sooner or later find himself in the realization of these desires, and all in accordance with natural laws and forces.

We are born to be neither slaves nor beggars, but to dominion and to plenty. This is our rightful heritage, if we will but recognize and lay claim to it.

One who never turned his back, but marched breast
forward,
Never doubted clouds would break,
Never dreamed, though right were worsted, wrong would
triumph,
Held we fall to rise, are baffled to fight better,
Sleep to wake.

Robert Browning

Will is the steady directing power: it is concentration. It is the pilot which, after the vessel is started by the mighty force within, puts it on its right course and keeps it true to that course.

Will is the sun-glass which so concentrates and so focuses the sun's rays that they quickly burn a hole through the paper that is held before it. The same rays, not thus concentrated, not thus focused, would fall upon the paper for days without any effect whatever. Will is the means for the directing, the concentrating, the focusing, of the thought-forces. Thought under wise direction,—this it is that does the work, that brings results, that makes the successful career. One object in mind which we never lose sight of; an ideal steadily held before the mind, never lost sight of, never lowered, never swerved from,—this, with *persistence*, determines all. Nothing can resist the power of thought, when thus directed by will.

To stand by one's friend to the uttermost end,
And fight a fair fight with one's foe;
Never to quit and never to twit,
And never to peddle one's woe.

George Brinton Chandler

The fearing, grumbling, worrying, vascillating do not succeed in anything and generally live by burdening, in some form or another, someone else. They stand in the way of, they prevent their own success; they fail in living even an ordinary healthy, normal life; they cast a blighting influence over and they act as a hindrance to all with whom they at any time come in contact. The pleasures we take captive in life, the growth and advancement we make, the pleasure and benefit our company or acquaintanceship brings to others, the very desirability of our companionship on the part of others—all depend upon the types of thought we entertain and live most habitually with.

No one could tell me where my Soul might be.
I searched for God but God eluded me.
I sought my brother out and found all there.

Ernest Crosby.

In the degree that we love will we be loved. Thoughts are forces. Each creates of its kind. Each comes back laden with the effect that corresponds to itself and of which it is the cause.

"Then let your secret thoughts be fair—
They have a vital part, and share
In shaping words and moulding fate;
God's system is so intricate."

If our heart goes out in love to all with whom we come in contact, we inspire love and the same ennobling and warming influences of love always return to us from those in whom we inspire them. There is a deep scientific principle underlying the precept—If you would have all the world love you, you must first love all the world.

It was only a glad "Good morning!"
As she passed along the way,
But it spread the morning glory
Over the livelong day.

By example and not by precept. By living, not by preaching. By doing, not by professing. By living the life, not by dogmatizing as to how it should be lived. There is no contagion equal to the contagion of life. Whatever we sow, that shall we also reap, and each thing sown produces of its kind. We can kill not only by doing another bodily injury directly, but we can and we do kill by every antagonistic thought. Not only do we thus kill, but while we kill we suicide. Many a man has been made sick by having the ill thoughts of a number of people centered upon him; some have been actually killed. Put hatred into the world and we make it a literal hell. Put love into the world and heaven with all its beauties and glories becomes a reality.

Not to love is not to live, or it is to live a living death. The life that goes out in love to all is the life that is full, and rich, and continually expanding in beauty and in power. Such is the life that becomes ever more inclusive, and hence larger in its scope and influence.

Give us men!
Strong and stalwart ones:
Men whom highest hope inspires,
Men whom purest honour fires,
Men who trample Self beneath them.

Men who make their country wreathe them
As her noble sons,
Worthy of their sires,
Men who never shame their mothers,
Men who never fail their brothers,
True, however false are others:
Give us Men—I say again,
Give us Men!

The Bishop of Exeter

Not repression, but elevation. Would that this could be repeated a thousand times over! *No, a knowledge of the spiritual realities of life prohibits asceticism, repression, the same as it prohibits license and perverted use. To err on the one side is just as contrary to the ideal life as to err on the other.* All things are for a purpose, all should be used and enjoyed; but all should be rightly used, that they may be fully enjoyed.

It is the all-around, fully developed we want,—not the ethereal, pale-blooded man and woman, but the man and woman of flesh and blood, for action and service here and now,—the man and woman strong and powerful, with all the faculties and functions fully unfolded and used, all in a royal and bounding condition, but all rightly subordinated. The man and the woman of this kind, with the imperial hand of mastery upon all,—standing, moving thus like a king, nay, like a very God,—such is the man and such is the woman of power. Such is the ideal life: anything else is one-sided, and falls short of it.

High thought and noble in all lands
Help me; my soul is fed by such,
But oh, at the touch of life and hands—
The human touch!
Warm, vital, close, life's Symbol dear,—

These need I most, and now and here.

Richard Burton

Thoughts of strength both build strength from within and attract it from without. Thoughts of weakness actualize weakness from within and attract it from without. Courage begets strength, fear begets weakness. And so courage begets success, fear begets failure. It is the man or the woman of faith, and hence of courage, who is the master of circumstances, and who make his or her power felt in the world. It is the man or the woman who lacks faith and who as a consequence is weakened and crippled by fears and forebodings, who is the creature of all passing occurences.

What one lives in his invisible thought world he is continually actualizing in his visible material world. If he would have any conditions different in the latter he must make the necessary change in the former. A clear realization of this great fact would bring success to thousands of men and women who all about us are now in the depths of despair. It would bring health, abounding health and strength to thousands now diseased and suffering. It would bring peace and joy to thousands now unhappy and ill at ease.

 I stay my haste, I make delays,
For what avails this eager pace?
I stand amid eternal ways,
And what is mine shall know my face

Asleep, awake, by night or day,
The friends I seek are seeking me;
No wind can drive my bark astray,
Nor change the tide of destiny—

The waters know their own, and draw

The brooks that spring in yonder height;
So flows the good with equal law
Unto the soul of pure delight.

The stars come nightly to the sky;
The tidal wave unto the sea;
Nor time, nor space, nor deep, nor high,
Can keep my own away from me.

John Burroughs

The thing that pays, and that makes for a well balanced, useful, and happy life, is not necessarily and is not generally a somber, pious morality, or any standard of life that keeps us from a free, happy, spontaneous use and enjoyment of all normal and healthy faculties, functions, and powers, the enjoyment of all innocent pleasures—use, but not abuse, enjoyment, but enjoyment through self-mastery and not through license or perverted use, for it can never come that way. Look where we will, in or out and around us, we will find that it is the middle ground—neither poverty nor excessive riches, good wholesome use without license, a turning into the bye-ways along the main road where innocent and healthy God-sent and God-intended pleasures and enjoyments are to be found; but never getting far enough away to lose sight of the road itself. The middle ground it is that the wise man or woman plants foot upon.

For evil poisons; malice shafts
Like boomerangs return,
Inflicting wounds that will not heal
While rage and anger burn.

Tell me how much one loves and I will tell you how much he has seen of God. Tell me how much he loves and I will tell you how much he lives with God. Tell me how much he loves and I will tell you how far into the Kingdom of Heaven,—the kingdom of harmony, he has entered, for "love is the fulfilling of the law."

And in a sense love is everything. It is the key to life, and its influences are those that move the world. Live only in the thought of love for all and you will draw love to you from all. Live in the thought of malice or hatred, and malice and hatred will come back to you.

And so love inspires love; hatred breeds hatred. Love and good will stimulate and build up the body; hatred and malice corrode and tear it down. Love is a savor of life unto life; hatred is a savor of death unto death.

"There are loyal hearts, there are spirits brave,
There are souls that are pure and true;
Then give to the world the best you have,
And the best will come back to you.

"Give love, and love to *your* heart will flow,
A strength in your utmost need;
Have faith, and a score of hearts will show
Their faith in *your* word and deed."

The kind of a man for you and me!
He faces the world unflinchingly,
And smiles as long as the world exists,
With a knuckled faith and force like fists:
He lives the life he is preaching of,
And loves where most is the need of love;
And feeling still, with a grief half glad,
That the bad are as good as the good are bad,
He strikes straight out for the right—and he
Is the kind of a man for you and me!

James Whitcomb Riley

After a certain age is reached in any life, the prevailing tone and condition of that life is the resultant of the mental habits of that life. If one have mental equipment sufficient to find and to make use of the Science of Thought in its application to scientific mind and body building, habit and character building, there is little by way of heredity, environment, attainment of which he or she will not be the master.

One thing is very certain—the mental points of view, the mental tendencies and habits at twenty-eight and thirty-eight will have externalized themselves and will have stamped the prevailing conditions of any life at forty-eight and fifty-eight and sixty-eight.

Who puts back into place a fallen bar.
Or flings a rock out of a traveled road,
His feet are moving toward the central star,
His name is whispered in the Gods' abode.

Edwin Markham

We need changes from the duties and the cares of our accustomed everyday life. They are necessary for healthy, normal living. We need occasionally to be away from our friends, our relatives, from the members of our immediate households. Such changes are good for us; they are good for them. We appreciate them better, they us, when we are away from them for a period, or they from us.

We need these changes to get the kinks out of our minds, our nerves, our muscles—the cobwebs off our faces. We need them to whet again the edge of appetite. We need them to invite the mind and the soul to new possibilities and powers. We need them in order to come back with new implements, or with implements redressed, sharpened, for the daily duties.

We need periods of being by ourselves—*alone*. Sometimes a fortnight or even a week will do wonders for one, unless he or she has drawn too heavily upon the account. The simple custom, moreover, of taking an hour, or even a half hour, *alone in the quiet*, in the midst of the daily routine of life, would be the source of *inestimable gain* for countless numbers.

I know not where His islands lift
Their fronded palms in air;
I only know I cannot drift
Beyond His love and care.

Whittier

We need more faith in everyday life—faith in the power that works for good, faith in the Infinite God, and hence faith in ourselves created in His image. And however things at times may seem to go, however dark at times appearances may be, the knowledge of the fact that "the Supreme Power has us in its charge as it has the suns and endless systems of worlds in space," will give us the supreme faith that all is well with us, the same as all is well with the world. "Thou wilt keep him in perfect peace whose mind is stayed on Thee."

There is nothing firmer, and safer, and surer than Deity. Then, as we recognize the fact that we have it in our own hands to open ourselves ever more fully to this Infinite Power, and call upon it to manifest itself in and through us, we will find in ourselves an ever increasing sense of power. For in this way we are working in conjunction with it, and it in turn is working in conjunction with us. We are then led into the full realization of the fact that all things work together for good to those that love the good.

Earth breaks up, time drops away,
In flows Heaven with its new day.

Browning

Milton Keynes UK
Ingram Content Group UK Ltd.
UKHW010628080324
438959UK00005B/369